W9-CNE-910

YOUR DIGESTIVE SYSTEM

Sally Hewitt

This library edition published in 2016 by Quarto Library., an imprint of QEB Publishing, Inc.

6 Orchard, Lake Forest, CA 92630

© 2016 QEB Publishing,
Published by Quarto Library., an imprint of Quarto Publishing Group USA Inc.

Distributed in the United States and Canada by
Lerner Publisher Services
241 First Avenue North
Minneapolis, MN 55401 U.S.A.
www.lernerbooks.com

A CIP record for the book is available from the Library of Congress.

ISBN 978 1 60992 878 0

Printed in China

Publisher: Maxime Boucknooghe
Editorial Director: Victoria Garrard
Art Director: Miranda Snow
Series Editor: Claudia Martin
Series Designer: Bruce Marshall
Photographer: Michael Wicks
Illustrator: Chris Davidson
Consultant: Kristina Routh

Words in **bold** can be found in the glossary on page 22.

Contents

Your food journey   4

Food energy   6

Into your mouth   8

Esophagus   10

Stretchy stomach   12

Small intestine   14

Liver and blood   16

Large intestine   18

Healthy digestive system   20

Glossary   22

Index   23

Next steps   24

Your food journey

When you eat, your food goes on a journey through your **digestive system.**

On the way, your body takes **nutrients** (the parts that are good for you) from the food. Then, your body gets rid of the parts it can't use.

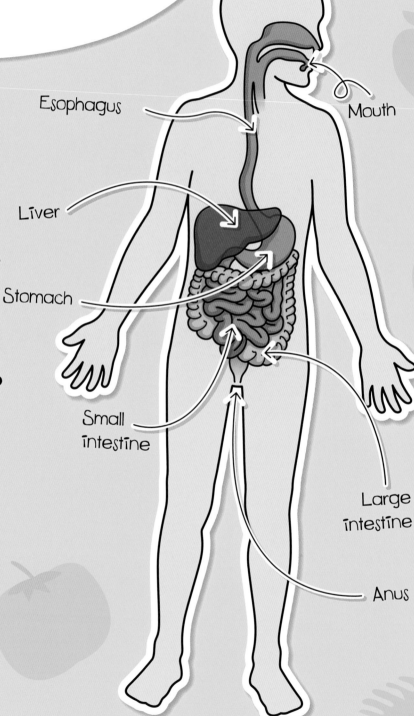

Esophagus

Mouth

Liver

Stomach

Small intestine

Large intestine

Anus

4

Activity

You will need scissors and pieces of string in four different colors. Cut each piece of string according to the following measurements:

Esophagus   10 inches (25 cm)
Stomach   8 inches (20 cm)
Small Intestine 23 feet (700 cm)
Large Intestine 5 feet (150 cm)

After the string has been cut, tie the pieces together. When you're fully grown, this is how far your food will travel!

Food energy

Food gives you **energy** to work, play, and grow. It helps to keep you warm and healthy. It's important to eat something from these four food groups every day.

1 Fish, meat, eggs, pulses, grains, and nuts help your body to grow and **heal**.

2 Bread, cereal, rice, and pasta give you the energy to keep going all day.

3 Milk, cheese, butter, and yogurt help to build strong bones and give you energy.

4 Fruit and vegetables are full of **vitamins** and **minerals** that keep you healthy. They also give you **fiber**, the rough part of food that helps your body to get rid of waste.

It is really important to drink plenty of water. Children should drink around 5-7 glasses a day.

7

Into your Mouth

Your food begins its journey in your mouth.

The look and smell of food can make you want to eat it. When you put food in your mouth, you taste it with the tiny **taste buds** on your tongue.

Your Mouth

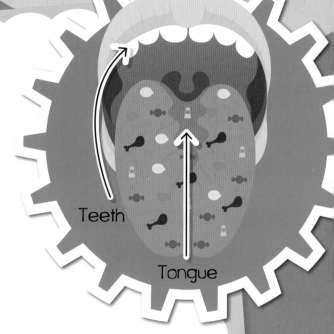

Teeth

Tongue

Activity

Smell your favorite dinner cooking. Feel your mouth water. It is filling with **saliva**, ready for eating!

You use your teeth to bite and chew your food into small pieces. Your front teeth are for biting. Your back teeth are for chewing.

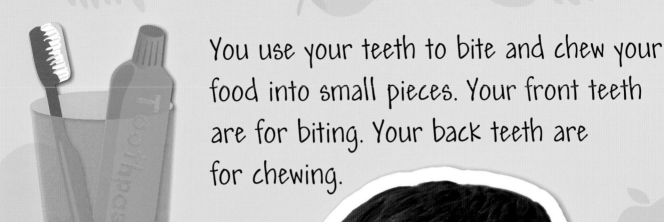

Look after your teeth. You need them for eating!

Saliva helps to digest your food and makes it easier to swallow. Your tongue also helps you to swallow your food.

Esophagus

When you swallow your food, it goes down a tube called the esophagus (say 'eh-sof-a-gus').

Your esophagus is next to your windpipe, which carries air to your lungs. A flap over your windpipe stops food from going down it.

Sometimes if you eat too fast, your food goes down the wrong way. That means it has gone down your windpipe by mistake! Try to eat slowly to avoid choking!

When you eat, muscles in your esophagus help push the food slowly down into your stomach.

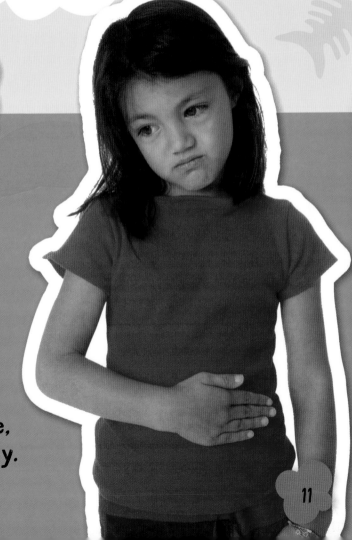

When giraffes bend down to drink, muscles in their esophagus push the water upward!

If you eat bad food, your body gets rid of it. Muscles squeeze the food back up again and you are sick.

▶ Being sick (vomiting) feels horrible, but it helps you to get better quickly.

Stretchy stomach

Your stomach is a muscle. It is like a stretchy bag. It stretches when it is full of food.

The walls of your stomach push food around. Food mixes with liquids in your stomach to make a thick soup that is easy to digest. This takes about three hours.

◀ After a big meal, you feel full.

When your food has turned runny like soup, it leaves your stomach. You start to feel hungry again when your stomach is empty.

Activity

Make a timetable of your meals. Notice the times when you feel hungry. Is it about three hours after your last meal? A healthy snack can stop you from feeling hungry between meals.

Breakfast	8 o'clock
Lunch	1 o'clock
Dinner	6 o'clock

Small intestine

After food leaves your stomach, it moves along into your small intestine. This is where it becomes even more runny and watery.

Activity

When your food is being digested, bubbles of gas in your intestines can make a rumbling sound. Have you ever heard your friend's tummy rumble? When a friend's tummy rumbles, see if you can put your ear on their stomach and listen!

Food is full of nutrients. Nutrients are the good things that your body needs to grow, keep healthy and have energy. While your food is in your small intestine, nutrients from it travel into your blood.

It's important to eat healthy food full of the nutrients your body needs.

Your small intestine is longer than your large intestine. It is called "small" because it is narrow.

Small intestine

15

Liver and blood

Blood takes nutrients from the small intestine to your liver. Your liver is the biggest **organ** in your body.

Your liver stores nutrients and gets rid of the parts of food that are bad for you. It makes a juice called bile, which breaks down nutrients into things the body can use.

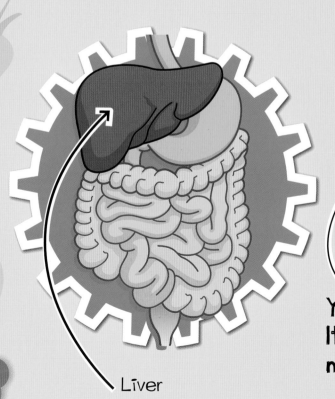

Liver

Your liver is like a cupboard. It gives you some food for now and stores some for later.

When your liver has done its job, it sends nutrients into your blood. Your blood then delivers goodness from your food to every bit of your body.

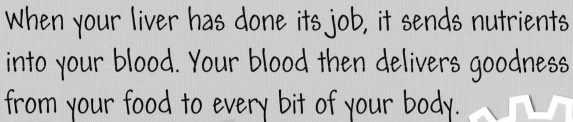

Your liver is one of the most important organs in your body!

Large intestine

When your food reaches the large intestine, it is mostly waste. Waste is the part of food that your body doesn't need. Food stays in your large intestine for about two days.

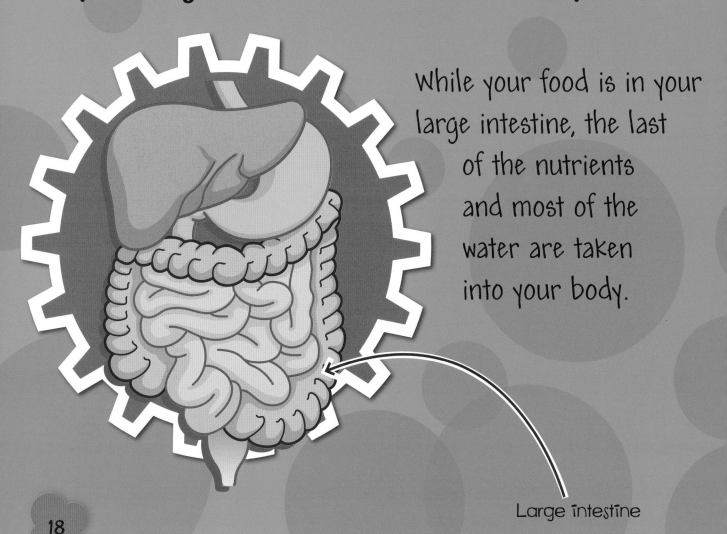

While your food is in your large intestine, the last of the nutrients and most of the water are taken into your body.

Large intestine

By the time the last of your food reaches the end of your large intestine, it has become "feces" (say "fee-sees"), which is the proper word for poop.

Your body gets rid of feces through an opening called the anus. Your food has reached the end of its journey!

Poop is what is left of your food after the goodness has been taken from it.

Healthy digestive system

There are lots of ways you can keep your digestive system healthy.

- Eat healthy food full of the nutrients your body needs.

- Drink plenty of water. It helps food travel through your digestive system.

Drink water with meals and when you're thirsty. Drink a bit more when it's hot or you are exercising.

- Try to eat lots of fruit and vegetables. They are delicious and help to make you strong and healthy.

▶ **Fruit and vegetables are full of fiber.**

Activity

Start the day with a breakfast that is good for your digestive system. Wash and grate an apple, including the peel. Slice a banana. Add milk, a little lemon juice, honey, and a sprinkle of oats. Mix it all together and gobble it down!

GLOSSARY

Digestive system

Your digestive system is all the parts of your body that digest food. When your body digests food, it mashes it up, uses the goodness, and gets rid of the waste.

Energy

Energy is what you need to give you the power to move, play, and work. Food gives you energy.

Fiber

The rough part of food that helps it travel through the digestive system.

Heal

Your body heals, or gets better, when you cut yourself or when you are ill.

Minerals

Minerals are tiny parts of goodness in food. Minerals in milk help you build strong teeth and bones.

Nutrients

Nutrients are the goodness in food that keeps you healthy.

Organ

An organ is a part of your body that does a special job. The liver is an organ that does the job of storing nutrients and cleaning your blood.

Saliva

Saliva is a liquid like water in your mouth. It helps you to taste and swallow your food.

Taste buds

Taste buds are bumps on your tongue. They tell your brain how your food tastes.

Vitamins

Vitamins are tiny parts of goodness in food. Vitamins in fruit help to keep your skin healthy.

INDEX

anus 4, 19

bile 16
blood 15, 16, 17

chewing 9, 10

digestion 12, 14

energy 6, 7, 15
esophagus 4, 5, 10, 11

feces (poop) 19
fiber 7, 21

gas 14

healing 6
healthy eating 6–7, 15, 20–21
hunger 13

large intestine 4–5, 15, 18, 19
liver 4, 16, 17

minerals 7
mouth 4, 7, 8, 9

nutrients 4, 15, 16, 17, 18, 20

saliva 8, 9
sickness 11
small intestine 4, 5, 14, 15, 16
stomach 4, 5, 11, 12–13, 14
swallowing 9, 10

taste 8
teeth 8, 9
tongue 8, 9

vitamins 7
vomiting 11

waste 7, 18, 19
water 7, 11, 18, 20
windpipe 10

NEXT STEPS

❁ Food gives us energy to work, play, and grow. Discuss other kinds of energy, such as gasoline for cars, and electricity for light. What happens to us without food, to a car without gas, and to a light without electricity?

❁ Lay out a variety of food and sort it into the main food groups (see pages 6 and 7). Discuss why your body needs each different kind of food.

❁ Draw a simple picture of the digestive system together (see page 4). Trace the route your food takes. Name each part the food is going through and describe what is happening to the food.

❁ Explain why it is so important to keep our teeth healthy. Eat a piece of crusty bread together. Point out how your front teeth bite, the pointed teeth tear, and the back teeth chew. Notice how teeth are the right shape for the job they do. Talk about the kind of food we would have to eat if we didn't have teeth!

❁ Create a stomach with a clear plastic bag. Pour a little orange juice into the bag to act as the "digestive juices." Add some bread to the bag and see what happens. Then squeeze the bag like the muscles in your stomach (make sure the bag is tied well!) Notice how the bread turns to liquid, ready to be absorbed into the small intestine and into the blood stream.